THE MUSTANG PROFESSOR:
THE STORY OF
J. FRANK DOBIE

THE MUSTANG PROFESSOR:
THE STORY OF
J. FRANK DOBIE

Written and illustrated by
Mark Mitchell

EAKIN PRESS ★ AUSTIN, TEXAS

To my wife, Marsha

FIRST EDITION

Copyright © 1993
By Mark Mitchell

Published in the United States of America
By Eakin Press / An imprint of Sunbelt Media, Inc.
P.O. Box 90159 ★ Austin, TX 78709-0159

ISBN 1-57168-134-5

3   4   5   6   7   8   9

Library of Congress Cataloging-in-Publication Data

Mitchell, Mark, 1951–
    The mustang professor : the story of J. Frank Dobie / by Mark Mitchell
        p.   cm.
    Includes bibliographical references.
    Summary: a biography of J. Frank Dobie, educator, writer, professor at the University of Texas, and collector of folklore of the Southwest.
    ISBN 1-57168-134-5
    1. Dobie, J. Frank (James Frank), 1888–1964 — Biography — Juvenile literature. 2. Authors, American — 20th century — Biography — Juvenile literature. [1. Dobie, J. Frank (James Frank), 1888–1964. 2. Authors, American 3. Folklorists.] I. Title.
PS3507.01833Z77   1991
818'.5209--dc20
[B]   91-18336
                                                                        CIP
                                                                         AC

Contents

Roundup

J. Frank Dobie (1888–1964) was more than an expert on rattlesnakes, cattle, stampedes, and mustang horses. He was a dynamic person who seemed to represent everything that was authentic, special, and good about Texas. His gift was making us appreciate the brilliance of our frontier heritage.

But Dobie was also a "disturbing influence," whose beliefs sometimes ran against the grain of a state that was stubbornly set in its ways. He waged a verbal war against plutocracy and blind conformity. He put himself in the front ranks of causes like equal rights, freedom of speech, and environmental protection — before the public realized these were causes.

The first book about J. Frank Dobie for young readers, *The Mustang Professor* traces Dobie's life from his childhood on a poor South Texas ranch to prominence as a writer and nationally recognized, Will Rogers-like celebrity. It introduces his two famous friends, the historian Walter Prescott Webb and the naturalist Roy Bedichek, who, with Dobie, came to be known as the "Texas Triumvirate" — central figures on the Texas literary scene.

In presenting this life of Dobie or "Pancho," as his friends called him (the Spanish nickname for Frank), *The Mustang Professor* also shares another unusual story. That story is of Texas and its largest university during crucial, formative years, as they struggled to shake off the frontier and enter "the modern age."

THE MUSTANG PROFESSOR:
THE STORY OF
J. FRANK DOBIE

1.

Brush Country Vaquero

It may have seemed like strange work for a former University of Texas English instructor. But J. Frank Dobie was glad Uncle Jim had given him the chance to drop out of teaching and go supervise work at the Los Olmos ranch.

Because he had grown up on a South Texas ranch, Frank had no trouble fitting in at Los Olmos. During his first week on the job, he roped a wild javelina and showed the *vaqueros* how to butcher and cook it for lunch. The *vaqueros* were impressed.

Frank always ached to be outdoors. Even though he was a college teacher, he felt more at home singing to cattle at night than he did studying in the university's tall library stacks. The rugged work on the range and the primitive life far away from the state capital suited him fine. From the branding, dipping, doctoring, and otherwise caring for thousands of head of cattle, to supervising the hands and paying the bills, Frank took charge of it all.

In the evenings, an old hand named Santos Cortez would drop by Dobie's cabin to chat. Cortez was a good *vaquero,* and the best storyteller on the ranch. Frank enjoyed Cortez's yarns about animals and *vaqueros* of long ago and ghosts who guarded buried Mexican treasure. He had heard similar tales as a child in Live Oak County.

The colorful things Cortez said reminded Frank of the rhymes his mother would use to roust him and his brothers and sister to church on weekends years before.

"Matthew, Mark, Luke, and John. Saddle the cat and all hop on," she would chirp at daybreak.

Frank could still picture the family piling into the wagon and making the long, bumpy journey to the little stone church in the Rameriena settlement. Families from all over the region would be there, and all of them knew the Dobie family as well as the Dobies knew them. The worshipers brought bedrolls and piles of food — fried chicken, potato salad, cornbread and biscuits, lemon and chocolate and coconut pies, large urns for boiled coffee. Church was a two-day affair.

Frank remembered watching his father, a quiet, unusually religious man in a plain suit and coarse white shirt, singing hymns as if he meant every word.

Frank never cared much for all the singing. He would rather be out riding his pony, Buck, chasing stray calves through the brush, or exploring the ruins of old Fort Ramirez on his family's acreage. The old fort had become nothing but a pile of rocks, but everyone said Spanish treasure from centuries gone by lay buried there somewhere.

Santos Cortez would talk of the past, and for Frank, the memories would rush in. He thought of the rough-hewn, one-room schoolhouse his father had built for him, his brothers, and sister, and the neighbor children on their property. He received his early schooling there.

When Frank and his sister Fanny were old enough to attend high school, they had to move to the town of Alice, Texas, to stay with their grandparents. Alice had the only high school in the whole region. It was Frank's first town.

More cattle were shipped from Alice than from almost any other location in the United States. Frank would go into town and watch cowboys work the great herds that were arriving. Near the stockyards loomed the largest pile of bones Frank had ever seen. He learned that companies bought the cow bones to grind them up into fertilizer and animal meal and sell to farmers. The mountain of bones, bleached white in the sun, made quite a sight in the middle of downtown.

Grandpa Dubose was Alice's justice of the peace and quite an Old West character. He had fought in the Civil War, driven wild horses, herded cattle, and even operated a stagecoach. He wore an old, broad-rimmed hat like the one settlers wore on the frontier. That hat was the last thing Grandpa Dubose took off before going to bed at night, after removing his vest, shirt, pants, shoes, and socks.

Grandma Dubose possessed a good education and had plenty of books for Frank and Fanny to read. She grew wild flowers and grasses all mixed together Mexican-style in front of her house.

Across the street lived a Texas Ranger captain. And a few blocks down, on the other side of the tracks, a Mexican bakery operated day and night. It filled the air with smells of rising bread and sweet pastries.

One night while Frank listened to Santos Cortez tell yet another of his ancient fables, Frank realized something. *Someday this will all be gone,* he thought.

He felt a rush of emotion.

Dobie would later write of his feeling that night: "While Santos talked, while Uncle Jim Dobie and other cowmen talked or stayed silent, while the coyotes sang their songs and the sandhill cranes honked their lonely music, I seemed to be seeing a great painting of something I'd known all my life . . ."

The "painting" he shared with Cortez, Uncle Jim, his wife and parents was not fancy. In fact, it was homely. The South Texas brush country was a universe of hard work and prickly brush, amazing silences and very few neighbors, but plenty of animals. Its legends of animals and weather, plants and trees, ghosts and devils, bees and rattlesnakes, cactus and superstition were unlike those of any other place.

As Texas grew "modern" like the rest of the nation, these strange, almost fairytale-like stories and the other unique qualities of a rural ranching culture would vanish forever. This secret, hidden life would be lost in the oncoming rush of civilization. Old-timers like Santos Cortez would not always be around to remind people about it.

Frank thought someone should try to save the pieces of the disappearing picture — before it was too late. He wondered. Should he return to the university to look into Texas lore and legends? Or should he stay on with the ranch foreman's job that he loved?

The cattle industry made the decision for him. The price of beef plunged, driving ranchers out of business all over the state. Conditions got so bad that Uncle Jim pulled him aside one day.

"Frank, I know I used to tease you about your schoolteaching," he said. "But maybe you had better go back. I may have to file for bankruptcy."

2.

Looking for Treasure — and Folklore

When Frank and his wife, Bertha, moved back to Austin, the University of Texas was the home of 4,000 students. Many of them were soldiers returned from the First World War. The campus was considered crowded. The state was so poor it could barely afford to build the wooden shacks and barracks in which the students would live and take classes.

Dobie barely paid attention. He was too excited about his ideas for teaching Texas "culture" that he had developed while at Los Olmos.

A literature class was as good a place as any for students to learn about their own environment, he decided.

Students of English literature were required to read poetry about "weeping willows, yellow daffodils, and nightingales." Why should they not also read about what was immediately around them, like "mesquite trees and coyotes and wild turkeys . . . and road runners?" Frank argued.

When he researched the state's libraries, he found very little written about such things. Texas was much too new and wild a place to have a written literature.

13

Frank was stumped. How would he provide his students with the Texas material he was talking about when there was so little published record, and no one had ever done such a thing before?

There was only one way. Frank climbed into his car and drove off. He would find more people like Santos Cortez to talk to him. He would personally gather all the lore about the state's past and its environment that he could. And he would lay the groundwork for poets and writers who wanted to say things about Texas.

While he was away, Bertha would teach his English classes for him.

15

Texas is a big state, and Frank traveled hundreds of miles. Wherever he went, he found people who wanted to tell him stories of the past. He collected folklore all around Texas and in New Mexico and Oklahoma too. He talked with old cowpunchers, range cooks, and traildrivers. He swapped tales with buffalo skinners and Indians on reservations.

In 1924 the university's Texas Folklore Society published its first book, *The Legends of Texas*. Most of the research and writing was done by Frank.

The editor of a national magazine, *The Country Gentleman,* asked Frank if he could write an article about cowboy songs. Frank knew just where he could find out all he needed to know about cowboy songs. His friend John Avery Lomax, another teacher at the university, was an expert on them. "I'll be glad to write the article," Frank said.

It wasn't long before Frank was the only University of Texas professor to be a popular magazine writer.

One day *The Country Gentleman* sent Frank to El Paso to interview an old treasure hunter. Frank met the man, C. B. Ruggles, for supper at a hotel. By the time the interview was over, both men got so excited talking about lost Spanish gold that they made up their minds to go prospecting — at once.

17

And they did. They spent the next several weeks riding muleback in northern Mexico, tracking down a place Ruggles had heard about called the Lost Tayopa Mine.

They traveled through lonely desert, camped under
the stars, and lived in Indian villages. The Indians
showed them old, deserted mines where their ancestors
had slaved, digging silver and gold for their Spanish
overlords.

Dobie and Ruggles found no treasure on this trip. And they did not find the mysterious, famous Lost Tayopa Mine. But Frank returned to Austin with what he was really looking for — lots of good stories about treasure and treasure hunters.

The more Frank wrote on the subject, the more people began to think of him as an expert on buried treasure. Treasure hunters accepted him as one of their esteemed peers. One father and son traveled all the way from Kansas to Austin to demonstrate their new invention to Frank: a "mine meter" for detecting underground riches.

Frank wanted to share with people more of the old folklore he'd been gathering. He proposed teaching a new course for the English Department. His title for the course was "Life and Literature of the Southwest."

"There is no 'literature of the Southwest,'" the faculty chairman said.

"Well, there's plenty of life. I'll teach that!" Frank replied.

Life and Literature of the Southwest became the most popular course offered at the university. Frank Dobie was its only teacher. Students crowded into class to hear his vivid stories of frontier life, cowboys, Indians, ranches, stampedes, dust storms, pioneer women, country music. No one had ever made the students' heritage more interesting for them.

3.

Frank Speaks His Mind

Meanwhile, Texas was beginning to attract scholars. Frank's friend Walter Prescott Webb, a history teacher at the university, wrote a book called *The Texas Rangers*. The book instantly became popular. No sooner did Webb finish that than he started to research pioneer life. Mody Boatright, another University of Texas English instructor, collected tales about the oil fields that had begun to spring up in East Texas.

Dobie decided to write a book about all the treasure hunters he had come to know about. Some, including those he had met, seemed a little crazy. One had given up digging in the mountains and had started to dig up his own yard and porch. He told Dobie he was sure Mexican silver was buried under there.

There was something a little sad about these isolated, eccentric characters who spent their lives questing for gold and silver. But Dobie believed it was just such people, driven by wild dreams of the glorious wealth they would find in the wilderness, who had conquered the West.

Dobie's book *Coronado's Children* was an overnight success. During the bleak days of the Great Depression,

CORONADO'S CHILDREN
by
J. FRANK DOBIE

when the public had almost no money to spend, Frank's saga of amazing hidden treasures found an eager audience.

No one had ever thought much of the Texas wilds before. Dobie was putting the region on the map. Now stories many Southwesterners had heard all their lives were being read with interest by people from all over the nation.

In the meantime, the University of Texas had stumbled on the luck that Dobie's characters only dreamed of. The Santa Rita Well No. 1 had struck oil on land owned by the university near Midland, in West Texas. Geologists had discovered a treasure that would make the university fabulously rich. The state's largest college would no longer have to rely on wooden shacks to house students and professors.

Dobie received a Guggenheim grant to collect folklore in Mexico. While Bertha taught his classes, Frank traveled to parts of Mexico no tourist had ever seen. When conditions got too rough to go by train or car, he hired a guide and traveled cross-country on burros. At night Frank and his guide slept on the ground. They hunted wild animals for food.

The land was lonely and strangely beautiful. He explored giant caves, their walls decorated with pictures that Indians had painted centuries ago. He visited ranches, remote villages, and early mining towns. He met more storytellers than he could count. They were old men — goat herders and *vaqueros* — who reminded him of home and Uncle Jim's ranch. Or they were grandmothers who knew how to heal the sick with herbs and magic.

He wrote a book on Mexico, *Tongues of the Monte* (voices of the mountain). It was filled with the strange folk stories he had heard on his travels in that country. But it did not sell well.

So he wrote another book, *Apache Gold and Yaqui Silver,* again about lost mines and treasures. It was successful right away, probably because of its subject.

The Dobies' home on Waller Creek, a few blocks from the university, attracted a lot of visitors. People would bring him artifacts: paintings of Western scenes, Bowie knives, powder horns, spurs, Mexican rugs, and always more maps to buried Spanish treasure.

On campus the students loved to visit Dobie. His office in B Hall was cluttered with cow skulls and animal hides. Ropes, whips, and riatas hung from the walls. As one writer later said, a visitor had to be careful where he or she sat in Frank's office. It might be on some steer horns!

Students swarmed Frank's Life and Literature of the Southwest class. Many wanted to hear him tell how, if they were ever lost in the brush country, they could survive off the fruit of the prickly pear cactus. The Spanish explorer Cabeza de Vaca had done so 400 years before.

And they liked hearing Frank Dobie speak his mind. When an Italian sculptor named Pompeo Coppini finished the statue at the Littlefield Fountain the university had commissioned him to do, Dobie examined it. Then he asked, "What has it got to do with Texas? A statue of a splay-legged, braying burro would have been more natural."

Coppini seemed to be the only sculptor around Texas at the time, though. Hired by the Texas Centennial Commission, he designed and built in downtown San Antonio a memorial to the fallen heroes of the Alamo.

Frank didn't understand that monument either. He told students it looked like a grain elevator. "The best thing about it is that you can't see it as you're going in the door of the Alamo," he said.

One day the university administration announced plans to use some of the school's new oil money to build new administration offices and a library. They decided to combine these all into one building that would be twenty-seven stories tall. It would be called the University Tower. Dobie was mystified. Why would the university, which spanned so many open acres, want to put up a skyscraper? he asked.

When students asked Dobie what he thought of the finished building, Frank shook his head. "It looks like a toothpick in a pie," he said.

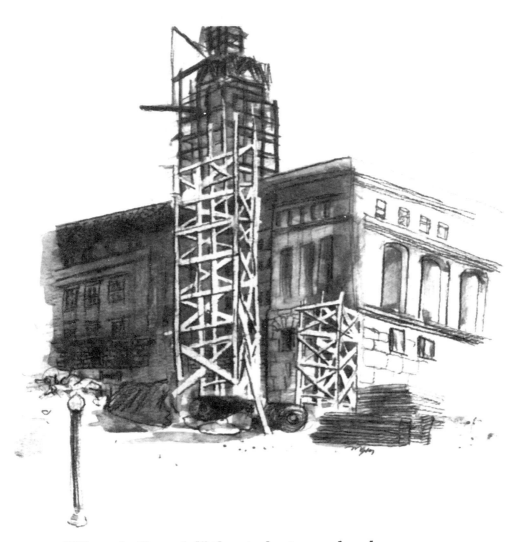

"What shall we do?" the students wondered.

"Maybe we can lay it on its side, put courtyards and flower beds around it," Dobie replied. Everyone laughed.

Then university officials announced that Dobie's own department would be moved into a top floor of the Tower.

Dobie refused to go.

While the other English professors packed up for the move, Frank did not budge from his old office at B Hall. So his faculty friends just left him alone there.

Sometimes his stubbornness got him into trouble, like the time he absolutely refused to pay a parking fine. He didn't believe the parking ticket he had received was fair. When the city judge could not persuade Dobie to pay the fine, he turned Frank over to the police.

Fortunately, Dobie did not have to go to jail. The chief let him work out his fine by doing chores around the police station.

Frank did not mind the controversy one bit. "I'm less worried about spending a night in jail than I am about all the Coppini statues [going up around] the Texas landscape," he told reporters who followed him around that day.

Reporters always quoted whatever he said.

When he had time, Frank still crossed the state by car, train, and pack mule in search of stories and folklore. As usual, whenever he was away from Austin, Bertha taught his classes for him.

As he usually did, Frank carried his bedroll with him on these trips, for sleeping outside. But now that more people knew Frank, or knew about him, there was never a shortage of places to stay. Friends in every corner of the state were only too happy to feed him and put him up for the night.

Dobie began to write a syndicated column for the newspapers. He called the column "My Texas."

People loved reading what Frank had to say. They loved it when he made fun of the changes in society brought by "progress." He would say things like, "I would sure rather hear a coyote bark than anything I've ever heard on another man's radio!"

Frank seemed to be popular whatever he did. Maybe readers liked the way he reminded them of a simpler time, before big machines and big business and the Great Depression took away some of the feeling that they controlled their own lives.

Frank decided his next book would be about Long-horn cattle and the lore that had developed about them. He began to study cattle. He read about the old cattle trail drives that grooved the earth between Texas, Kansas, and Missouri during the 1870s. He thought of that huge, white pile of bones and the stockyards he had watched for hours as a teenager in Alice.

He drove up to the Panhandle and stayed with the legendary cowman and traildriver Charles Goodnight for a few days.

Goodnight was a crusty old man by then, but his memories of pioneer life were as fresh as if the incidents had happened the day before. He talked about driving cattle through lightning storms and blinding blizzards, about fighting Comanches and bad men. And, hard and crusty as he was, Goodnight liked talking to Frank about these things.

Frank was having a great time. Nothing beat re-searching the history of the Longhorns.

But his mother felt something was not quite right.

"Why are you always looking backward, son?" she asked him one day. "You're acting like an old man."

39

40

4.

Talking Politics and Visiting England

Frank's friends included some of the most original thinkers at the university. Every afternoon at five, Dobie would sit out in his backyard and wait for visitors to show up.

Professor Walter Prescott Webb, by that time a famous historian, would drop by. Following him would come Roy Bedichek, who ran the university's Interscholastic League competitions and spent his spare time studying plants and birds.

Mody Boatright, the folklorist, would often pop up. And, in later years, Joe Small, the editor of *True West* Magazine, and Frank Wardlaw, the director of the new University of Texas Press, visited often. Young teachers like Joe Frantz and students like John Henry Faulk would ring the doorbell.

And that was how it was for the rest of Dobie's life. Anybody who wanted to could drop by Frank Dobie's house in the early evenings. They would find a lot of people in the backyard, talking, exchanging ideas, and telling stories. After a couple of hours, Bertha would come out and shoo everyone home so Frank could eat his supper. Frank would talk all night if nobody stopped him.

But Frank started doing less talking and more listening. His mother's attitude troubled him. Did she mean that he was living in the past more than he should? Was he missing something important now?

Frank's friends complained about how the state was being led by narrow, profit-minded businessmen. The governor, W. Lee "Pappy" O'Daniel, owned a flour mill in Fort Worth. He had become famous as the announcer of a country music show on the radio. His company had sponsored the show. People had voted for him because he seemed so nice on the radio. But, as governor, "Pappy" seemed to listen only to the rich people.

Meanwhile, the oil that the university continued to draw from its West Texas lands was making it one of the richest institutions in the world. Governor O'Daniel appointed some very cautious men to run the university. These administrators were called regents. They weren't professors like Dobie and Webb. They were successful businessmen and ranchers. They felt as O'Daniel did — that a university's main job was to train people for work. In the regents' opinion, that work should be good for the economy of Texas: the oil industry, railroads, agriculture, and manufacturing. They wanted engineers, managers, scientists, and technical specialists.

The regents did not trust new ideas, including the changes being made by President Franklin Roosevelt in his New Deal programs. The New Deal was the president's attempt to pull the country out of the Depression by hiring thousands of people to work on public projects.

"Pappy" and the regents didn't like the New Deal. It reminded them of Communist Russia. Government shouldn't meddle in people's affairs, they believed. Texas could take care of itself.

Just as they disliked Roosevelt, the regents didn't care much for the University of Texas president. His name was Homer Rainey.

Rainey was a professor. But he had also once played professional baseball. He was an individual. The regents didn't like him because he let professors who had a wide variety of beliefs, values, and backgrounds teach at the university.

As a younger man, Rainey had been ordained as a Baptist minister. On Sundays, he liked to preach at churches around town. He told folks how they needed to work together to build a better world.

The regents weren't happy with Rainey's sermons. They thought the world was fine as it was — if only the New Dealers and the Communists would leave it alone.

While Rainey was not liked by the regents, he was very popular with the people who gathered in Dobie's backyard every night. Dobie listened to his friends. And it was clear to him that they were worried about what was happening at the university.

But Frank had work to do. To finish *The Longhorns,* he secluded himself on an island off the Gulf Coast. The ranch house he stayed in had no telephone and could only be reached by ferry.

The Longhorns contains all kinds of stories about the cattle he had known as a child. Included is the true story of Sancho, the homesick steer. Cowboys had driven Sancho all the way from Kerr County, Texas, to the wilds of Wyoming. But Sancho missed his old ranch so much that he walked away from the herd one day. Nobody missed him. He kept walking until he was back in his own pasture in Texas.

The Longhorns was Dobie's most popular book. And then something pushed it from the public's mind: World War II.

Military dictators who had troubled different parts of the globe in recent years brought it on. Nazi Germany invaded France. Japanese planes bombed Pearl Harbor in Hawaii. It looked as if America would have to enter the war.

England and the United States would fight the war on the same side. To make it easier for the countries to work with each other, England asked a few American professors to teach British soldiers about Americans and American life. Someone recommended Frank Dobie, and Frank was invited to go to England.

Frank got an uncharacteristic case of stage fright. "I haven't read the United States Constitution since I was a boy, and I didn't understand it then!" he argued.

"I know the average length of horns on a Longhorn steer. I can tell you how mother rattlesnakes swallow their young. I can tell you about the duels Jim Bowie fought with his knife . . . But I don't know history."

"Sounds like American history to us," the English told him.

Dobie's good friend Walter Prescott Webb was already in England, teaching at Oxford University. "Make your own definition of history and come on over," Webb wrote Frank.

The British soldiers were eager to learn every detail about their new allies. As the new visiting professor of American history at Cambridge, Dobie did not want to disappoint them. "Never in my life have I so dreaded making an appearance before a new class," he wrote Bertha.

To keep up with his students, he had to study harder about America than they did.

England was going through a dangerous time. Its
people lived in the thick of war. Nazi Germany was
trying to conquer the country. Nazi planes dropped
bombs on its cities and menaced its countryside.

Frank got used to air raids, like everyone else there.
He learned to turn off his lights at night so that enemy
planes could not see his apartment as they flew over it.

Frank felt sympathy for the people of England.
When he wasn't teaching soldiers, he visited bomb shel-
ters, hospitals, and train stations. He toured the ranches
and poked his head inside old cathedrals, tiny pubs, and

47

the busy parliament. He kept making friends with people — not just professors and scholars at Cambridge, but business folks, laborers, government workers, air wardens, doctors, nurses, farmers, and gardeners. He felt close to them because of the hardships they endured.

Somehow the difficult conditions made people kinder to each other. Making friends was easy. It reminded Frank of South Texas.

Frank was never lonely at Cambridge, although it was thousands of miles away from home. "So many people ask me to tea and dinner that I have to keep a calendar," he wrote Bertha.

Edward R. Murrow, the famous American war correspondent, would later say of Dobie during this time, "He did more to win British respect and affection than our entire diplomatic corps and propaganda campaigns combined."

Dobie learned in England that the world was too small to hide in. Society's immediate challenges had to be faced. Sitting in front of a campfire in Mexico and losing oneself in old folk fables was no different from hiding in a library. His mother was right. From now on, Frank would try harder to belong to the modern world.

At the graduation ceremony at Cambridge, the dons presented Frank to the university senate as "the sombrero-wearer among the men in togas." They then awarded him an honorary master's degree. The diploma said, *"De bobus longicornibus quod ille non cognivit, inutile est allis cognoscere."* The Latin words meant, "What he does not know about Longhorn cattle is not worth knowing."

Dobie read his diploma and beamed.
Meanwhile, there was trouble in Texas.

5.

Trouble at the University

The University of Texas regents had fired Homer Rainey, its president. Rainey had refused to remove "offensive" books from the university library. He had also refused to fire three economics professors who had spoken out against America's role in the war.

Students and many professors objected to Rainey's dismissal. In a protest against the regents, they marched up Congress Avenue to the state capitol. In their march, they carried a coffin, which symbolized the "Death of Academic Freedom."

When Dobie returned from England to the United States, he, too, was upset. He stopped in New York City and spoke before a group of former University of Texas students.

Why, Frank said, it looked like the regents were trying to control thought at the university the same way the Nazis had tried to control Europe! Was this the American way? he asked.

Now that the university was unbelievably rich and had powerful and rich friends in Washington, D.C., and all over, was it afraid of freedom and new ideas? Dobie asked.

Frank's remarks before the New York group reached Austin, and people frowned at them. Frank was calling the regents Nazis. Had he been listening to Communists while he lived in England? they wondered.

This was not the first time since he'd left for England that Frank had raised eyebrows. Texans were suspicious when he wrote in his newspaper column, "My Texas," that labor unions should be allowed to organize strikes — even during war. Business leaders said strikes would interfere with the war effort. The Texas legislature had outlawed them. Many Texans did not believe workers should organize for any reason.

So what was Frank Dobie doing calling for strikes?

His column got a lot of attention. The United Auto Workers Union liked it so much that they reprinted it as a pamphlet and mailed it to union workers all across the country.

Now that Frank was back in Austin, he was asked about this.

Frank said he believed that strikes were sometimes a good idea. The first strike in Texas was in the 1880s and was organized by hard-working cowboys, he pointed out. They wanted better working conditions and slightly better pay.

"I understand that," Dobie said.

But Dobie's answer didn't satisfy everyone. Some of his cowboy friends sidled up to him. "Frank, are you sure you're not a Communist?" they whispered.

"No!" Dobie responded. He just hated to see wealth and power making bullies out of people, he said.

As Texans mulled that over, Frank picked another issue to be unpopular about.

He wondered why blacks had never been allowed into the University of Texas. He had seen black students in his classes at Columbia University in New York City, when he was a graduate student. In Texas, though, African-Americans always attended schools far removed from white students. The black schools were underfunded and almost always substandard.

As World War II ended, a serious young black man named Heman Marion Sweatt applied to attend the University of Texas Law School. When he was turned down, Sweatt filed a lawsuit against the university. The state responded by creating another law school — one just for African-Americans. It was in Houston, in a one-room class located above a saloon.

Sweatt refused to attend this "law school." He pressed on with his suit against the university.

Frank heartily applauded Sweatt's stand.

"I am for admitting blacks to the university at once," Dobie told an audience of several thousand black residents in East Austin. "I am for equal opportunity for Negroes in Texas. I know that keeping one's fellow man down in ignorance is evil and undemocratic."

The new governor, Coke Stevenson, called Frank a "disturbing influence." Organizations that had invited Dobie to talk about his experiences in wartime England canceled their invitations. Texans who had supported Frank Dobie throughout his career turned their backs on him now.

He received letters telling him that he should have died after writing *Apache Gold and Yaqui Silver*. He had made a better account of himself back then, they said.

What had got into J. Frank Dobie? He had made Texans proud once. Nobody knew how to do that better than he.

This, after all, was Texas' golden era. For the first time the state was enjoying tremendous political and economic power in the nation. Texas practically bragged of winning World War II by itself, with all the oil and gasoline it produced. The state had provided nearly one-tenth of the American soldiers who fought in the war.

"I get belly tired of Texas bragging," Dobie wrote a friend. "The truth is, I felt freer in England than I feel in this land of the free and home of the brave."

When the U.S. War Department asked him to return to Europe to keep company with American troops, Dobie agreed. He wanted to get away from Austin for a while.

He toured American army camps in England, Austria, and Germany. In Germany, he spoke at Red Cross clubs in Frankfurt, Munich, and Vienna. Wherever he went, the troops packed around to hear him talk. He always cheered them up. Frank was also seeing up close the results of the war. He was in Nuremberg while the captured Nazi leaders were being tried there for terrible war crimes.

Frank returned to Texas after a year. He wanted to research rattlesnakes, he said. "They make better company than the governor of Texas," he explained.

When he asked the university for another leave of absence, so that he could write, the university refused to give it to him. The regents and the new university president, Theophilus Shickel Painter, were mad at him. Frank had already been away too long, they said.

Frank's friend Walter Prescott Webb smelled trouble brewing. He knew that Frank would be out of a teaching job, and the university would lose its greatest celebrity, if relations between Frank and the regents weren't patched up fast. Webb tried to talk to the regents.

At Webb's urging, Dobie paid a visit to President
Painter. But Dobie and the new university president
found they had little to say to each other.

Before the day was over, everyone on campus knew
J. Frank Dobie had been dismissed. The regents had refused to renew his teaching contract. Outraged students
marched in a long column to Dobie's house. They carried
banners and chanted, "We want Dobie!"

Dobie came out of the house to thank them.

"You're the best professor who ever got on a horse," they said.

"Well, that's kind of you. But don't worry about me," Dobie said. "I'll be around here if any of you ever need me. I'm not going anywhere.

"And as long as my books are still in the university library, I'll still be 'teaching.'"

Frank promised that his door would always be open to students. And if they needed an article written for *The Daily Texan* (the student newspaper) about Texas' folklore or current events, they could call on him.

6.

Last Roundup for an Old Cowboy

In the evenings, Frank continued to sit in the back-yard with his old university friends. He still loved hearing Roy Bedichek talk. Bedichek was the oldest of his group of friends and the most learned man Dobie had ever known.

Driving anywhere with Bedichek would take twice as long as driving with anyone else. Bedi, as he was called, would notice things in the landscape — a rock, or a plant, or the grass. He would stop the car and get out to take a look and then talk about it.

Ancient civilizations and their philosophies interested Bedi as much as wildlife did. He liked to get up every morning at three to read classical Greek literature. It put him in the mood he needed to read the newspapers that came at sunrise, he said.

Dobie and Webb took turns telling him, "Bedi, you know so much. Do you realize if something were to happen to you, all of your knowledge would be lost to the world? You need to write a book."

Dobie took up a collection and raised enough money for Bedi to take several months off. Then they dropped him off at Webb's Friday Mountain ranch to live in solitude for a change. "Now get busy and write," they instructed him.

For the next two months, Bedi didn't write anything. He was too busy noticing all the plants and the twisted oak trees and the grasses and animal life around him. As usual, he stopped to look at everything. He picked up weeds and sod clumps and pebbles and would turn them over and think about them.

Finally, he went into the cabin and wrote his book. It was the first book he had ever written in his life. Bedichek was seventy-one years old. His book, *Adventures with a Texas Naturalist*, immediately was hailed as a classic.

Now all three friends — Bedichek, Dobie, and Webb — were famous authors.

In the summer, Dobie and Bedi and anyone who cared to join them braved the icy waters of Barton Springs. Students could usually find them out at Bedi's rock, swimming small laps or sitting in the sun, talking seriously to each other. Webb did not join them on these occasions. He didn't want students to see him in his swimming trunks.

One day a new statue was placed on campus: Phimister Proctor's sculpture of running mustangs. Now here was a statue that reflected Texas! Dobie had taken a hand in it. When Proctor began work on the project years before, Dobie drove him to a friend's ranch so he could see for himself what wild mustangs really looked like.

Dobie had long admired mustangs. Indians long ago had stolen the Arabian-blooded horses from corrals all over Mexico and Texas. Horses that broke away from the Indians roamed South Texas until it resembled a sea of wild ponies. The wild spirit of these mustangs made them beautiful.

Eventually, settlers moved in. The mustangs found their prairie hemmed in by fences and windmills. Their grass was reserved for sheep and cattle. Soon the ranchers were shooting them as if they were varmints. The mustangs almost vanished from the earth.

But Proctor's statue had brought them back.

"I wish we had another one as good of Longhorns," Dobie said at the dedication.

Dobie's reputation as a "disturbing influence" continued to dog him. In Washington, the U.S. House Committee on Un-American Activities announced that he belonged to a Communist group. The group was the Mid-Century Conference For Peace.

Dobie resented the accusation. If one or two members of the group happened to be Communists, he didn't know it, he said. He apologized for not investigating each member of a group whose cause he believed in.

When the legislature set up a "textbook committee" to screen and censor textbooks, Dobie marched to the capitol to tell legislators what he thought about that. People jammed the galleries to hear him.

"A censor is always a tool," Dobie said that day. "Not one censor in history is respected by enlightened men of any nation.

"Any person who imagines he has a corner on the definition of Americanism and wants to suppress all concepts to the contrary . . . is an enemy of the free world . . ."

Throughout these and other controversies, Dobie continued to gather stories. He had finished a book about mustangs and was now researching one on old cowboys. He talked to old cowboys on ranches, in nursing homes, around campfires, and at the lobby of the old Menger Hotel in downtown San Antonio.

He sat down with old cowboys wherever he could find them. And even the most button-mouthed old wrangler would open up to him. As one writer said, Dobie had a way of listening that would make a post want to talk.

But Frank could not help but notice something in his search for old cowboys: They were getting harder and harder to find. They had seemed as common as cactus once. Now they were as rare as horned lizards. In fact, they were just about gone.

One day Frank's mother died, and all that was left of the old family ranch in Live Oak County was sold to Houston investors.

Frank closed his eyes. In his mind, he was eleven again, riding home on his horse, Buck.

The land was quiet. There were no cars in that part of the world. They had hardly been invented. There were no cities around. Just miles and miles of brush and mesquite, cactus and rock, and isolation so complete it was spooky.

He halted Buck by a water trough under the windmill to let him drink. He enjoyed the sound of Buck swallowing. He listened to frogs croak around them. In an oak tree down by the creek, a large owl boomed out *whoot-whoot-whoot.*

Frank answered the owl. "I cook for myself. Who cooks for you-all?" he called out with a cupped hand, in the way his father had taught him to answer the owls. That is what owls say, his father had told him.

A coyote in the valley cornfield yelped.

Frank's dog, Joe, near the house gallery, barked sharply.

Frank rode Buck through the yard up to the house. He heard the gate slap the gatepost, and from the open kitchen window, a voice. "Is that you, son?"

His mother had been watching for him.

Glossary

appoint — to select a person to fill an office or position.

bankruptcy — a legal action taken when someone no longer has the money to pay off debts.

censor — to examine written material and remove information that seems improper to the person who is censoring.

communism — In a communist system, the state owns everything. The state is expected to provide all people with what they need to survive: food, shelter, health care, and clothing. To many, this opposes American ideals of democracy and personal freedom. In Dobie's day, many Americans feared that Communists were trying to start a revolution to take over this country, as they had done in Russia in 1917.

controversy — a dispute between people who have different views.

correspondent — a person employed by a newspaper or the media to provide news.

culture — the arts, beliefs, and institutions of a particular people.

Depression — a period of severe economic hardship; the period in America after the fall of the stock market in 1929.

dictator — a person who is granted (or who takes) complete and absolute power over a government.

don — what Cambridge and Oxford universities call professors.

faculty — a branch of teaching in a school or university, or the teachers in that particular branch (as in the English faculty or Math faculty).

folklore — traditional customs, tales, or sayings preserved among a group of people. Often these are not in writing.

javelina — a wild boar.

justice of the peace — a person in the state court system who is elected to oversee minor cases.

lawsuit — when there is argument about whether an action is legal, the case is taken before a court.

menaced — threatened.

Nazi — a member of the National Socialist German Workers' Party, which came to power under Adolf Hitler.

New Dealer — a person who supported President Franklin Roosevelt's New Deal program of social and economic reform during the 1930s. Many Texans distrusted the federal government becoming too involved in their lives and businesses, and therefore distrusted the New Deal.

pamphlet — a printed publication smaller than a book, with no cover or a paper cover.

parliament — a body of representatives who have power over legislation.

peers — persons who have a similar situation as another person (as in age, class, etc.).

primitive — something as it was originally.

regents — the people who rule or govern a university; similar to a board of directors.

riata — a lariat (rope).

rural — having to do with the country, not the city.

strike — when employees stop working in order to get their employers to listen to a problem.

substandard — below what is considered acceptable.

union — an organization of workers.

unique — different from any other thing.

vaquero — cowboy; particularly a cowboy of Spanish or Latin-American descent.

Sources

These books by J. Frank Dobie:

Apache Gold and Yaqui Silver. Boston: Little, Brown, 1939.

Coronado's Children. Austin: The University of Texas Press, 1978.

The Longhorns. Boston: Little, Brown, 1941.

The Mustangs. Boston: Little, Brown, 1952.

Some Part of Myself. Edited by Bertha McKee Dobie. Boston: Little, Brown, 1980.

Tales of Old Time Texas. Boston: Little, Brown, 1955.

A Texan in England. Boston: Little, Brown. 1945.

Tongues of the Monte. Garden City, New York: Doubleday, Doran, 1935.

Other books:

Abernethy, Francis Edward. *J. Frank Dobie.* (Vol. 1 of the Southwest Writers Series.) Austin: Steck Vaughan Company.

Bode, Winston. *J. Frank Dobie: A Portrait of Pancho.* Austin: Pemberton Press, 1965.

Caro, Robert. *Path to Power.* New York: Vintage Books, 1983.

Dugger, Ronnie (editor). *Three Men in Texas.* Austin: University of Texas Press, 1967.

Fehrenbach, T. R. *Lone Star: A History of Texas and Texans.* New York: American Legacy Press, 1983.

Handbook of Texas: A Supplement. Vol. 3. Austin: Texas State Historical Association, 1976.

McMurtry, Larry. *In a Narrow Grave.* (The chapter "Southwestern Literature?") Austin: Encino Press, 1968.

Powell, Lawrence Clark. *Books in My Baggage.* (The chapter "Mr. Southwest.") Cleveland: World, 1960.

Tinkle, Lonnie. *An American Original: The Life of J. Frank Dobie.* Boston: Little, Brown, 1978.

University of Texas Ex-Students Association. *The Ex-Students History of the University of Texas in Pictures*. Austin: University of Texas Press, 1970.

Yarborough, Ralph. *Dobie: Man and Friend*. Washington, D.C.: Potomac Corral of the Westerners, 1967.

Interviews:

Joe Frantz, professor of history at Corpus Christi State University, former Walter Prescott Webb Distinguished Professor of History at the University of Texas.

Special thanks to Joe Frantz; Ed Eakin; Katherine Gee, curator of art and the Dobie Collection at the University of Texas Humanities Research Center; Barbara Hood and Bill Arhos of KLRU-TV; and the staffs of the Humanities Research Center and the Barker Texas History Center at the University of Texas at Austin.

ABOUT THE AUTHOR/ILLUSTRATOR

MARK MITCHELL is a freelance reporter and illustrator whose articles have appeared in *American Artist, The Washington Journalism Review, Highlights For Children, Texas Highways,* and many other publications. He has illustrated stories for *Pockets,* a children's magazine, and several books.

Mitchell graduated from the University of Texas at Austin with a B.S. in radio, television and film. Later he worked as reporter and city and business editor for *The Williamson County Sun* in Georgetown, Texas, where J. Frank Dobie, as a student at Southwestern University, had cut his teeth as a writer nearly eighty years earlier.